TALKABOUT Sound

TALKABOUT
Sound

Text: Angela Webb
Photography: Chris Fairclough

Franklin Watts
London/New York/Sydney/Toronto

© 1987 Franklin Watts
12a Golden Square
London W1

ISBN: 0 86313 564 1

Consultant: Henry Pluckrose
Editor: Ruth Thomson
Design: Edward Kinsey

Typesetting: Keyspools Limited

Printed in Hong Kong

About this book

This book has been written for young children—in the playgroup, school and at home.

Its aim is to increase children's awareness of the world around them and to promote thought and discussion about topics of scientific interest.

The book draws on examples from a child's own environment. The activities and experiments suggested are simple enough for children to conduct themselves, with only a little help from an adult, using objects and materials which will be familiar to them.

Children will gain most from the book if the book is used together with practical activities. Such experiences will help to consolidate knowledge and also suggest new ideas for further exploration and experimentation.

The themes explored in this book include:

Sound can be made in many different ways.
Sound is made by vibrations.
Sound ceases when vibrations stop.
Sound travels through air as sound waves.
Sound also travels through water and solid objects.
Sounds can be high and low.
Sound echoes in certain situations.

Do you enjoy making sounds?

What sounds do these things make
if you bang them?

What different sounds
can you make with your body ...

and your voice?

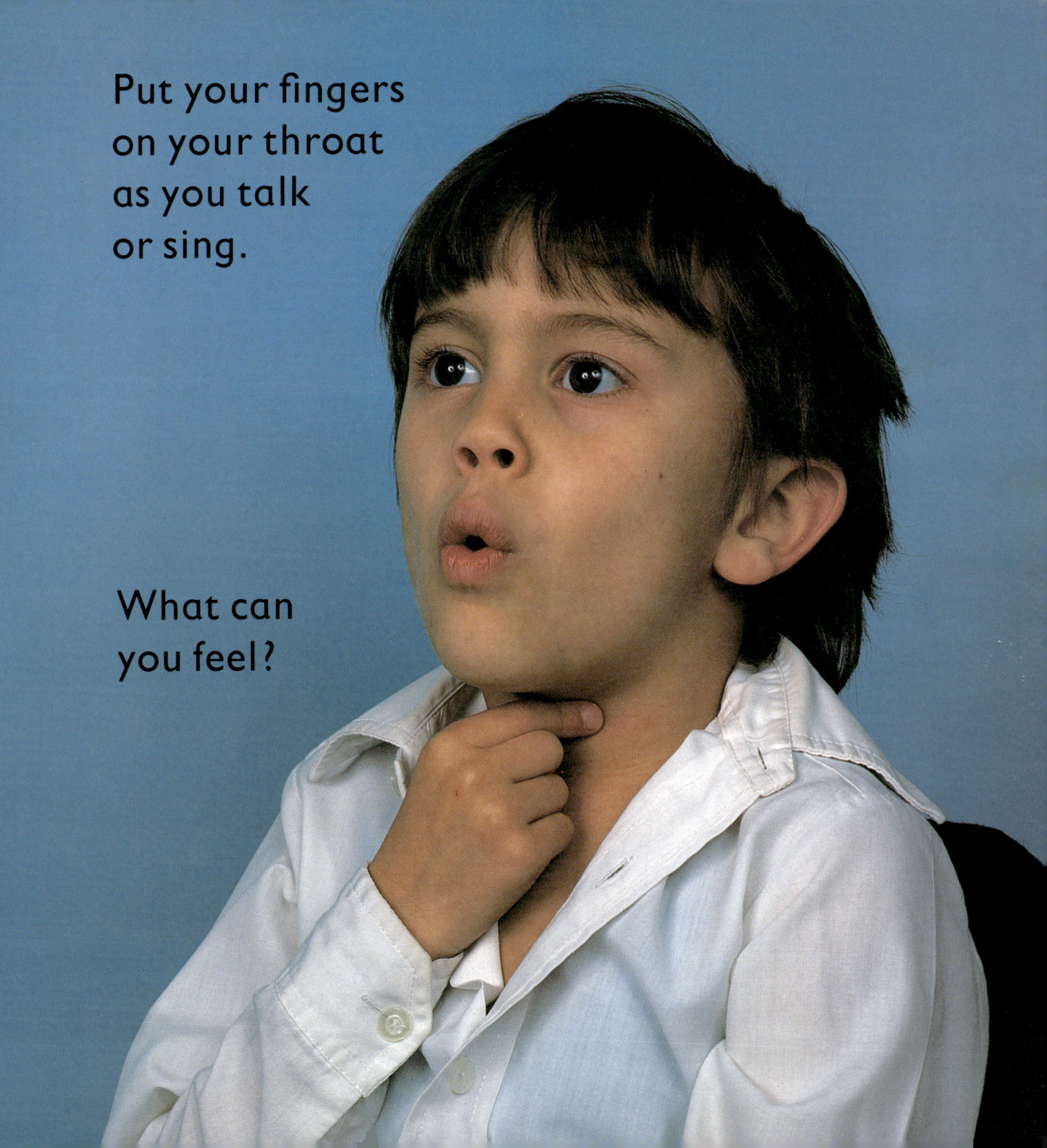

Put your fingers
on your throat
as you talk
or sing.

What can
you feel?

Hold a ruler on the edge
of a table.
Press down the end
and let go.

Can you hear a sound?
What do you see?

Whenever you hear a sound
there is something moving.
This movement is called a vibration.

Try this with a rubber band and see.

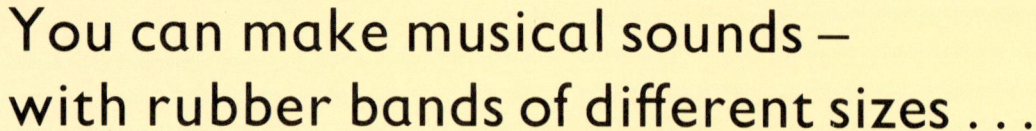

You can make musical sounds —
with rubber bands of different sizes . . .

or by plucking
the strings
of a guitar.

Strike a triangle with a beater.
Touch the triangle while it is ringing.
What can you feel?

When something stops vibrating, the sound stops.

How does
someone's voice
reach you?

The sound travels
through the air
as sound waves.

Throw a stone in a pool of water. Watch how the waves spread out. Sound waves move through the air in a similar way.

Cup your hands round your ears
when you're listening to music.

Does the music sound louder?
You are catching more sound waves.

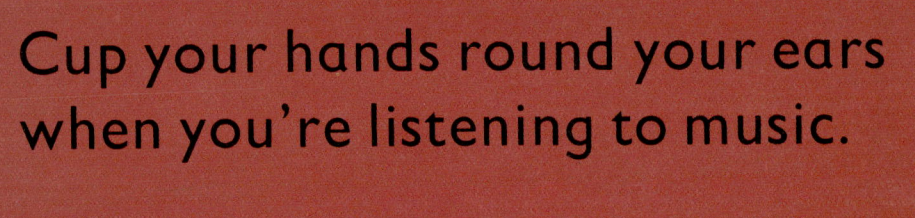

How well can you hear on a windy day?

Wind can blow sound waves away.

Sound also travels through water.

Put your ears under water.
What can you hear?

How well does sound travel
through solid things?

Put your ear against one end
of a plank.

Can you hear
if someone taps
the other end?

Does sound travel through the slack string of a yoghurt pot telephone?

What happens if the string is stretched tight?

If you shout in a tunnel the sound bounces back.

What is this called?

How can you use a tube
to help you hear
from further away?

Can you hear if someone speaks
through a narrow tube?

Try it again with funnels
stuck in both ends.
How does the sound change?

How can you make your voice sound louder . . .

or softer and more muffled?

Some sounds are high.
Others are low.

Which of these bottles
will make highest
if you bang them?

What do you notice about the sounds the long and short nails make?

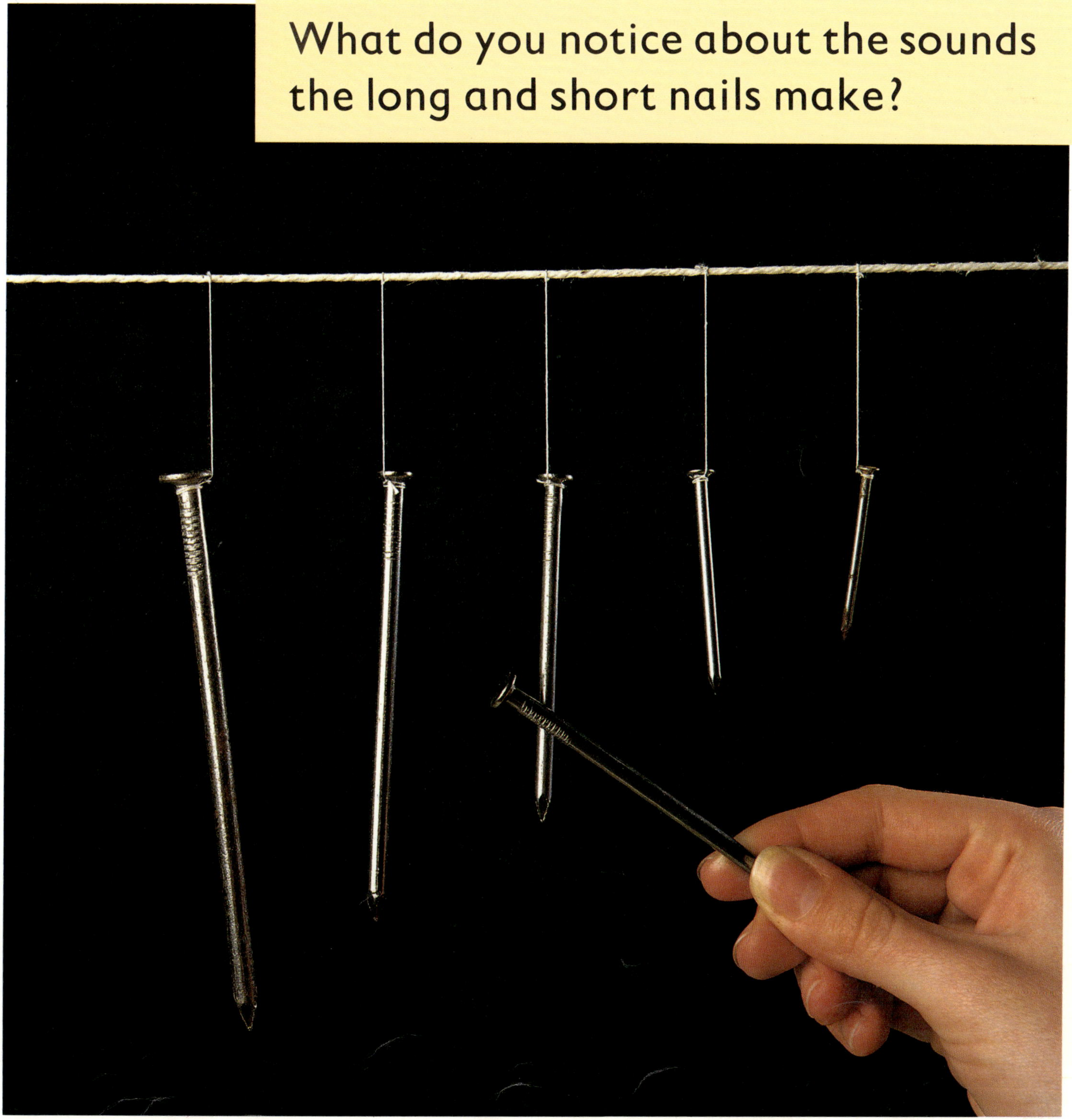

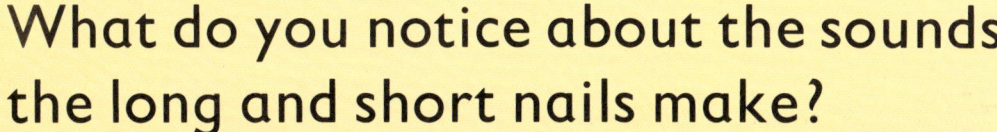

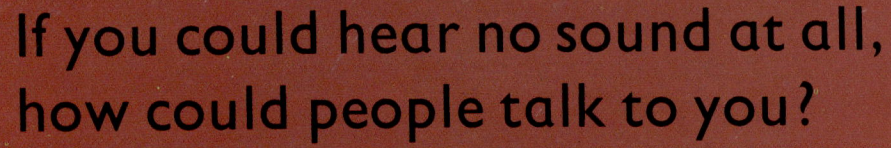

If you could hear no sound at all,
how could people talk to you?